Contents

Zhang Heng

Multi-talented Chinese scholar Zhang Heng was an astronomer, mathematician, painter, writer, and poet. He is best known for inventing the **seismograph**.

Earthquake detector

Zhang Heng was chief astrologer of the Han Dynasty in Ancient China. One of his jobs was to record earthquakes. He invented the seismograph, shown top left. This machine detects the underground waves of an earthquake.

Find out more

Search for more about Zhang Heng at: www.chinaculture.org

Learn about earthquakes at: www.earthquakes.bgs.ac

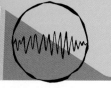

Timeline

Becomes an official at the imperial court

Zhang's seismograph detects an earthquake 800 km (500 miles) away

78	116	132	138	139

Zhang born in Nanyang, China

Invents the seismograph

Zhang dies

Ptolemy

The Greek astronomer and geographer Ptolemy explained the movement of the stars and planets, and drew a world map used for centuries after his death.

The Ptolemaic System

Ptolemy assumed that the Earth was at the centre of the universe. He then used maths to describe the movement of the stars and planets. His theory was not accepted until more than one thousand years later.

Find out more

A summary of Ptolemy's discoveries can be found at: http://obs.nineplanets.org/psc/theman

Timeline

Born in Alexandria, Egypt

Ptolemy dies

c. 90	c. 150	c. 168

Almagest written

Nicolas Copernicus

Polish astronomer and mathematician Nicolas Copernicus challenged ideas that had been accepted for centuries. He thought that the Sun was at the centre of universe.

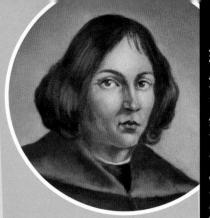

A religious life

Copernicus became convinced that planets move around the Sun. He worked out that the Earth moves around the Sun once a year. He also realized that the Earth spins as it moves. This makes the stars move across the sky and makes it light in the morning and dark at night.

Copernicus was 18 when he started his studies at university in Krakow, Poland. It was there that his love for astronomy began. Copernicus became a **diplomat** when he left university. At the same time, he developed his ideas about the universe. His ideas spread among Europe's astronomers. He published his theory in a book called *On the Revolutions of the Heavenly Bodies* in 1543.

What he said

❝ Finally we shall place the Sun himself at the centre of the Universe. ❞

How did he die?

Copernicus died from a stroke soon after he saw the first printed copy of his book.

Timeline

Born in Toruń, Poland		Becomes a priest at Frauenburg Cathedral	The Catholic Church finally lifts its ban on Copernicus's work	
1473	**1491**	**1497**	**1543**	**1835**
	Goes to University of Krakow		Publishes a book on the movement of the planets just before he dies	

Find out more

Find out more about Copernicus at www.visittorun.pl

Learn more about astronomy at www.kidsastronomy.com

Start of a revolution

Most astronomers who read Copernicus's work did not believe him. They continued to follow Ptolemy, who thought that the Earth was at the centre of the universe (⇨p4). Copernicus also got into trouble with the Catholic Church. The Church thought that God created the Earth at the centre of the universe, and it banned his book. Centuries passed before astronomers started to believe in the Copernican system.

Galileo Galilei

Italian mathematician and astronomer Galileo Galilei made many discoveries about the planets and stars, and about the motion of objects on Earth.

What he said

66 … in the discussion of natural problems we ought to begin … with experiments… 99

Did you know?

Galileo experimented with falling objects by dropping weights from the Leaning Tower of Pisa.

Find out more

The Galileo Project site:
http://galileo.rice.edu/galileo.html

Find out more about Galileo and his work at:
www.thespacesite.com/space_galileo_astronomy

Galileo's work

Galileo gave up studying medicine when he developed a passion for mathematics. He carried out experiments with falling objects. In 1583, after watching a swinging lamp in Pisa cathedral, he realized that a **pendulum** (a string with a weight attached) always takes the same time for each swing. He used this idea to design a pendulum clock.

Timeline

1564	1581	1610	1632	1632	1642
Born in Pisa, Italy		Builds a telescope and studies space	Publishes a book criticizing Ptolemy's ideas		Dies near Florence, Italy, aged 77
	Begins medical studies at Pisa			Put under house arrest	

Galileo discovered Moon craters, **sunspots**, and realized that the Milky Way was made up of stars. He found four of Jupiter's moons (now called the Galilean moons), which led him to support Copernicus (⇨p5). In 1632, he published a book saying that Ptolemy was wrong (⇨p4). He was put on trial by the Catholic Church and placed under house arrest for the rest of his life.

Place in science

Galileo overturned many theories that had been accepted for hundreds of years, such as Aristotle's theory that heavier objects fall faster than lighter ones (⇨p19). Galileo was one of the first scientists to use experiments to test his theories. His work helped the scientific revolution of the 16th and 17th centuries.

Johannes Kepler

German mathematician and astronomer Johannes Kepler is best remembered for his theories on how the planets move.

Early interest in space

Kepler was a brilliant mathematician from an early age. After university and work as a mathematics lecturer, he was invited to Prague by the famous Danish astronomer, Tycho Brahe. Brahe was mathematician to the Holy Roman Emperor Rudolph II. When Brahe died a year later, Kepler took over his position.

Kepler used Brahe's records on astronomy to find out more about the movement of the planets. Eventually, he realized that the planets move in ellipses (squashed circles) around the Sun, not in perfect circles. Kepler published his ideas in two books in 1609 and 1619. The books summarized his ideas about how the planets moved.

What he said

66 … the earth is round, and is inhabited on all sides; it is insignificantly small… 99

Find out more

This site is all about Johannes Kepler:
www.johanneskepler.com

Read more at:
http://galileo.rice.edu/sci/kepler.html

www.hps.cam.ac.uk/
starry/kepler.html

Timeline

1571	1600	1601	1609	1619	1630
Born near Stuttgart, Germany	Becomes mathematician to Emperor Rudolph II		Publishes his second book		
		Invited to Prague by Tycho Brahe	Publishes his first book		Dies, aged 58, in Regensburg, Germany

Kepler's place in science

Kepler's breakthrough in astronomy was to realize that planets move in ellipses. He used mathematics to predict the movements of the planets. His predictions matched the real movement of the planets. Kepler's work supported Copernicus's view that the planets move around the Sun (⇨p5). It also helped future astronomers to predict the positions of the planets.

Did you know?

At the age of six, Kepler saw the spectacular Great Comet of 1577.

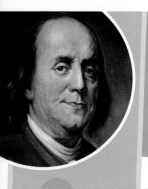

Benjamin Franklin

Benjamin Franklin ran a printing business and played a major role in American independence. He also made important discoveries about electricity.

Stormy science

In 1748, Franklin sold his successful printing business to fund his scientific research. In 1752, he deliberately flew a kite in a thunderstorm to prove that lightning is a form of electricity. This led to his invention of the **lightning conductor**.

Find out more

Find out more about the Franklin's life at:
www.ushistory.org/franklin/info

Timeline

Carries out his famous kite-flying experiment

Becomes American ambassador to France

| 1706 | 1752 | 1776 | 1776–1785 | 1790 |

Born in Boston, USA

Signs the Declaration of Independence

Dies in Philadelphia, USA, aged 84

Charles Lyell

Charles Lyell, a Scottish lawyer whose hobby of **geology** became his career, supported an idea that the processes that shape the Earth happen over millions of years.

History in rocks

Lyell was Professor of Geology at King's College in London. He studied volcanoes, **glaciers**, rock formations, and fossils. His major theory was that we can tell what happened to rocks in the past by looking at rock formations today.

Timeline

Born in Kinnordy, Scotland

Publishes a book about his theories

| 1797 | 1816 | 1830 | 1875 |

Leaves Oxford University

Dies and is buried in Westminster Abbey, London

Alfred Wegener

German **meteorologist** Alfred Wegener found evidence that the Earth's continents were once joined together, but his ideas were not accepted until thirty years after his death.

Wegener's supercontinent

Wegener studied astronomy at the University of Berlin, Germany. He moved on from studying astronomy to become an expert in meteorology, the scientific study of the weather. Wegener was also interested in earth sciences. In 1911, he found evidence that fossils in rocks on opposite sides of the oceans matched each other. He believed that about 250 million years ago the continents we know today were joined in one supercontinent. He named it Pangaea, which is Greek for "all land". Since then, the continents have moved slowly apart. He published his theories in 1915.

What he said

66 … earth sciences must contribute evidence toward unveiling the state of our planet in earlier times. 99

How did he die?

Wegener died while on an expedition to Greenland in 1930.

Timeline

Born in Berlin, Germany

Publishes his ideas

| 1880 | 1911 | 1915 | 1930 |

Finds evidence of continental drift

Dies, aged 50

Find out more

The University of California Museum of Paleontology gives a biography of Wegener at: www.ucmp.berkeley.edu/ history/wegener.html

A theory rejected

Wegener could not prove that the continents were moving or even say why they were moving. As a result, most people rejected the idea. He was finally proved right in the 1960s, decades after his death, when scientists found places where the ocean floor was spreading outward. This discovery led to the theory of **plate tectonics**. This theory suggests that forces deep within the Earth's core cause events such as earthquakes and mountain formation.

Edwin Hubble

American astronomer Edwin Powell Hubble discovered that there are other **galaxies** outside our own, and that the universe is much larger than previously thought.

What he said

66 Equipped with his five senses, man explores the universe around him and calls the adventure Science. 99

How did he die?

Hubble died from a blood clot in his brain.

Find out more

A site dedicated to Hubble with lots of images and quotes:
www.edwinhubble.com

The Franklin Institute Science Museum website has more information:
www.fi.edu/learn/case-files/hubble

Finding galaxies

Hubble studied astronomy and mathematics at the University of Chicago, USA. He went on to study law at Oxford University. After fighting in World War I, he started work at Mount Wilson Observatory in the United States. Using what was then the most powerful telescope in world, he studied nebulae (clouds of dust in space). In the early 1920s, he realized that many so-called nebulae were in fact galaxies of stars outside our own galaxy. This discovery made him famous. Hubble continued to study galaxies and found that they are moving away from us. This showed him that the universe is expanding. Hubble continued working at Mount Wilson until his death in 1953.

Timeline

1889 — Born in Missouri, USA

1919 — Joins Mount Wilson Observatory

1925 — Discovery of other galaxies is made public

1953 — Dies, aged 63

The Big Bang

Astronomers once believed that all the objects in space were collected together in our galaxy, the Milky Way. Following Hubble's discovery, the universe turned out to be millions of times bigger than astronomers thought. It also supported the Big Bang theory – that the universe started with a huge explosion 15 billion years ago and is still growing. The Hubble Space Telescope is named after Hubble in recognition of his work.

Stephen Hawking

Theoretical physicist Stephen Hawking is famous for his work on **black holes** and the origins of the universe, and for his best-selling science books.

Hawking's theories

Hawking was not a brilliant pupil at school, but he still won a place to study physics and mathematics at Oxford University. He went on to study cosmology (the science of the universe) at Cambridge University. While at Cambridge he was diagnosed with motor neurone disease, which can affect movement and speech and gets worse with time. At first he was given just a few years to live. He is now in a wheelchair with very little movement left. He speaks through a computer using a simulated voice.

What he said

"… we can understand the Universe. That makes us something very special. **"**

Find out more

Hawking's official website includes an autobiography:
www.hawking.org.uk

Black holes are explained through an animated site at:
http://hubblesite.org/explore-astronomy/black-holes

Timeline

1942	1963	1974	1979	1988

Born in Oxford, England — 1942

Diagnosed with motor neurone disease — 1963

Becomes a fellow of the Royal Society in London — 1974

Becomes Lucasian Professor of Mathematics at Cambridge University — 1979

Publishes *A Brief History of Time* — 1988

During the 1970s, Hawking came up with the theory that the universe began as a single point in space have no size but they are incredibly dense. These points are called singularities and they are found at the centre of black holes. Hawking suggested that the universe will end up as a collection of black holes.

Popular books

Apart from his scientific papers, Hawking has also written books for the general public, including *A Brief History of Time: From the Big Bang to Black Holes*, which became a best-seller. It has allowed general readers to understand some of Hawking's complex ideas about the universe.

Did you know?

Hawking is trying to unify the two great theories of physics – general relativity and **quantum theory**.

Anton van Leeuwenhoek

Looking through his new microscopes, Dutch cloth merchant Anton van Leeuwenhoek discovered **micro-organisms** such as **bacteria** and **protozoa**.

What he said

66 ... I have thought it my duty to put down my discovery on paper, so that all ingenious people might be informed thereof. 99

Did you know?

Van Leeuwenhoek found a way to make perfect lenses but died before passing on his method.

A lens maker

Van Leeuwenhoek was born in Delft, in the Netherlands, and lived there all his life. He started working as a draper (worker in the cloth business) when he was 16, and a few years later had built up his own business. He later worked in Delft's law courts.

Timeline

Born in Delft, in the Netherlands		Discovers bacteria		Dies, aged 90
1632	**1674**	**1683**	**1684**	**1723**
	Discovers protozoa		Discovers red blood cells	

In his spare time, van Leeuwenhoek learned how to make lenses. His lenses were more powerful than any made before, and he used them in microscopes that could magnify objects up to 300 times. In 1674, he discovered single-celled organisms, called protozoa, that live in water, and then bacteria in 1683. In 1684, he made another important discovery – **red blood cells**.

The father of microbiology

Nobody had ever seen the micro-organisms that van Leeuwenhoek discovered with his microscope, and so he is often called the "father of microbiology". We now know that many bacteria and protozoa cause infections and diseases. Van Leeuwenhoek made this link between micro-organisms and illness. He made hundreds of microscopes, but only nine of them exist today.

Robert Hooke

English scientist Robert Hooke studied in many different areas of science, including astronomy and physics, but is best known for discovering plant cells with his own microscopes.

Partnership with Boyle

Hooke worked as assistant to Robert Boyle (⇨p21). In 1659, he devized the first air pump to create the **vacuums** needed for Boyle's experiments. In 1662, Boyle helped Hooke get a job at the Royal Society in London. Hooke stayed at the Royal Society for the next 40 years. During this time he invented the compound microscope (shown top right), which has two lenses. This gave better magnifications and clearer images than single-lens microscopes. Hooke used his microscopes to look at natural objects, such as wood and fossils. He observed the tiny building blocks that make up plants and animals and came up with the word "cell" to describe them. In 1665, Hooke published *Micrographia* (which means "small drawings" in Latin). This contained detailed drawings of what he saw through his microscopes.

What he said

66 ... the science of nature has been already too long made only a work of the brain and the fancy. 99

Did you know?

The only known portrait of Hooke went missing in 1710 and has not been found since.

Timeline

Born on the Isle of Wight, England	Starts work at the Royal Society in London	Dies, aged 67

| 1635 | 1656 | 1662 | 1665 | 1703 |

Starts partnership with Robert Boyle in Oxford	Publishes *Micrographia*

Find out more

This site includes pictures of Hooke's architectural work:
www.roberthooke.org.uk

Find out more about the important events that shaped Hooke's life:
www.roberthooke.com

Hooke's legacy

Among his achievements were the discovery of the law of **elasticity**, called Hooke's Law, and the discovery that materials expand when they are heated. As well as the microscope, Hooke also developed other instruments, such as the telescope and meteorological devices.

13

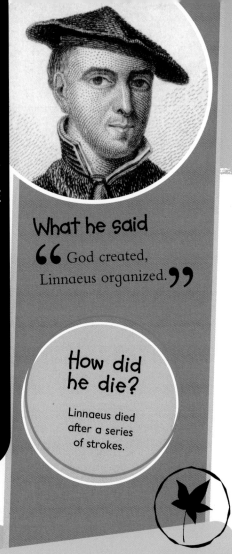

Carl Linnaeus

Carl Linnaeus, a Swedish botanist and physician, developed a logical system for classifying the natural world. Scientists still use it today.

What he said

66 God created, Linnaeus organized. 99

How did he die?

Linnaeus died after a series of strokes.

Classifying the world

Linnaeus's interest in plants and their names came from his father, who was a keen gardener. As part of his studies, Linnaeus collected plants that were used as medicines. Linnaeus moved from Sweden to the Netherlands to finish his studies. All the time, he was working on a way to classify animals and plants by their characteristics. He published his system, called *Systema Naturae,* for the first time in 1735. Linnaeus returned to Sweden in 1738 to practise medicine. He later became doctor to the Swedish royal family.

Linnaeus travelled the world in search of new animals and plants to classify. He also sent students on trips to various parts of the world. The first edition of *Systema Naturae* was just 11 pages long. By the end of his life, the book was made up of several volumes. Linnaeus managed to classify more than 4,400 species of animals and 7,700 species of plants.

Find out more

Discover more about Linnaeus at:
www.linnaeus300.com

The Natural History Museum page:
www.nhm.ac.uk

The Linnean Society: www.linnean.org

Timeline

Born in Stenbrohult, Sweden

Dies in Sweden, aged 70

1707   **1735**   **1778**

Moves to the Netherlands and publishes *Systema Naturae*

Leaving a collection

During his life, Linnaeus gathered a huge collection of animal and plant specimens. A few years after his death, the collection was sold to an English historian who then founded the Linnaean Society. The collection contains over 40,000 specimens and is housed in London.

Charles Darwin

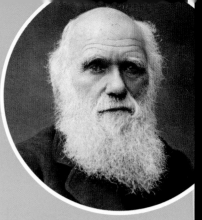

In the 1830s, English biologist Charles Darwin came up with his revolutionary theory of plant and animal **evolution**. This theory was called "survival of the fittest".

Darwin's voyage

Darwin studied medicine and religion at university but became interested in nature. So he left university to become a naturalist aboard HMS *Beagle* on a voyage to South America and the islands of the Pacific. At the Galápagos Islands, Darwin noticed that animals and plants of the same species on different islands had slightly different body features.

What he said

"... man still bears in his bodily frame the indelible stamp of his lowly origin. **"**

Timeline

Born in Shrewsbury, England

Publishes *On the Origin of Species*

Dies in Downe, England, aged 73

| 1809 | 1831–1836 | 1859 | 1871 | 1881 |

Works as naturalist on HMS *Beagle*

Publishes *The Descent of Man*

Find out more

This site includes a biography, timeline, and pictures:
http://darwin-online.org.uk

A website dedicated to the life and times of Charles Darwin:
www.aboutdarwin.com

In the following years, Darwin realized that different body features developed to help animals and plants adapt to life on each island. Helpful adaptations passed on to the next generation of animals and plants. Darwin called this process "natural selection". He thought that it was the driving force behind evolution. In 1859, Darwin published a book called *On the Origin of Species by Means of Natural Selection*.

Darwin's legacy

Natural selection explains how tens of thousands of different species have evolved to live on our planet. Darwin's theory was not generally accepted for many decades because it is against the beliefs of the Church.

How did he die?

Darwin died after a series of heart attacks.

Johann Gregor Mendel

Austrian monk Johann Gregor Mendel is recognized as the "father of **genetics**", but his work about inheritance in plants was not appreciated during his lifetime.

The monk

Mendel formed the basis of the science we now know as genetics by studying pea plants. His work was forgotten until many years after his death, when other biologists realized its significance.

Find out more

The latest about Mendel's life and work: www.biography.com/scientist.html

Timeline

1822	1856	1866	1884
Born in Heinzdorf, now in the Czech Republic	Starts experiments with pea plants	Publishes *Experiments with Plant Hybrids*	Dies, aged 61, from a kidney infection

---

Alfred Russel Wallace

The English naturalist Alfred Russel Wallace came up with the idea that species change over time. Only the fittest species can adapt to the changes and survive.

Research

Wallace travelled the world collecting specimens of animals and plants. He realized that different species change over time. Some of the changes help species to survive, but some do not. In 1857, Wallace discovered he shared the same theory as Charles Darwin (⇨p15).

Find out more

Discover more about Wallace at: www.strangescience.net/wallace.htm

Timeline

1823	1848–1852	1854–1862	1858	1913
Born in Usk, Wales	Travels to the Amazon to collect insects	Expedition to Asia	Makes his theory of natural selection public	Dies, aged 90

Rosalind Franklin

During her short life, English scientist Rosalind Franklin never got the credit she deserved for her discoveries about the structure of **DNA** – the chemical that holds our genetic information.

Working alone

After gaining a degree in chemistry from Cambridge University, Franklin worked in London and Paris. In Paris she learned a technique called **X-ray** diffraction, which helps to show how atoms are arranged in crystals. In 1951, she moved to King's College, London, where she was asked to work out the structure of DNA (deoxyribonucleic acid). Using X-ray diffraction, Franklin discovered that DNA comes in a spiral shape called a helix.

Franklin did not get on well with one of her colleagues, Maurice Watson, and worked alone. In 1953, Watson showed Franklin's work to Francis Crick and James Dewey Watson (⇨p18), who were also studying DNA. It helped them to work out a model for DNA. When they published their findings, they did not give credit to Franklin.

What she said

66 By doing our best we shall succeed in our aims: the improvement of mankind. 99

Find out more

Search for more about Franklin at:
www.accessexcellence.org

Read about Franklin's life involvement in DNA study:
www.dnai.org

The Rosalind Franklin Papers:
http://profiles.nlm.nih.gov.uk

Timeline

Born in London, England

Describes the structure of DNA

1920   **1951**   **1952**   **1958**

Begins studying DNA

Dies in London, England

Franklin recognized

DNA carries the genetic information in every plant and animal cell. Finding its structure was a major achievement in the science of genetics. Franklin's role in discovering its structure is now recognized. It is possible that she was not given credit at the time because she was a woman in a world that was dominated by male scientists.

How did she die?

Franklin died from cancer in 1958, aged just 37, after two years of illness.

Crick and Watson

Englishman Francis Crick and American James Dewey Watson worked out the structure of DNA – the chemical that holds our genetic information. They won a Nobel Prize for their work.

What they said

66 The moment I saw the picture my mouth fell open. 99

(James Watson)

How did he die?

It is said that Crick was still editing a scientific manuscript when he died.

Forming a partnership

Crick (on the right) and Watson (on the left) met at the Cavendish Laboratory in Cambridge, England, where they shared an office. They both had an interest in DNA and decided to piece together its structure. They worked out that a DNA molecule is long and thin and has a sort of backbone, but they could not work out the exact structure.

In 1953, Crick and Watson saw some X-ray diffraction photographs produced by Rosalind Franklin (⇨p17) and given to them by Franklin's colleague, Maurice Watson. The photographs showed that DNA was a helix shape, like a long, twisted spiral. Franklin's photographs were the last piece of evidence they needed. Soon, Crick and Watson had built a model of the DNA molecule. The two scientists became famous almost overnight.

Find out more

Read about the lives of Crick and Watson at:
www.bbc.co.uk/history/historic_figures/watson_and_crick.shtml

Read more at the DNA Interactive site at:
www.dnai.org

Timeline

Francis Crick born in England

Watson and Crick join forces at Cambridge

Francis Crick dies, aged 88, in California, USA

1916 **1928** **1951** **1953** **2004**

James Dewey Watson born in Chicago, USA

The pair work out the structure of DNA

Place in science

Crick and Watson showed that DNA has a double helix shape, like a twisted ladder, so the molecule can make copies of itself by unzipping along its length. The discovery was so important that Crick and Watson shared the 1962 Nobel Prize for Medicine with Maurice Watson.

Aristotle

Greek philosopher Aristotle studied every subject known in Ancient Greece. He is best remembered for his ideas in science. His theories were believed for thousands of years.

The five elements

Aristotle was born into the Greek aristocracy. When he was 18, Aristotle went to Plato's Academy in Athens, Greece. He studied with Plato (c. 427–347 BC) for 20 years. Aristotle based his theories on his observations of nature. He believed that everything on the planet was made up of four elements: earth, fire, air, and water. For example, he thought that all rocks were made of the earth element.

Aristotle came up with the idea of a fifth element, called aether, which he believed made up the Sun, Moon, planets, and stars. He believed that the Earth was at the centre of the universe, with the Sun, Moon, planets, and stars moving around it. When Plato died, Aristotle left Athens and travelled to Asia, where he became Alexander the Great's teacher. He returned to Athens in 335 BC to begin his own school, the Lyceum. He fled Greece after the death of Alexander, fearing for his life.

What he said

" No great genius has ever existed without some touch of madness. "

Did you know?

It has been said that Aristotle was the last person in history to know all there was to know.

Find out more

This site includes a general overview of Aristotle's life and work.
www.historyforkids.org/learn/greeks/philosophy/aristotle.htm

Another useful site.
www.philosophypages.com

Timeline

Aristotle born	Becomes Alexander the Great's teacher		Dies in Euboea, Greece
c. **384** BC	**367–347** BC **342** BC	**335** BC	c. **322** BC
	Studies at Plato's Academy	Founds the Lyceum school	

A long-lasting legacy

Aristotle's theories were believed for nearly 2,000 years. Scientists only started to challenge his ideas when science underwent a major revolution in the 16th century.

Archimedes

A Greek mathematician, scientist, inventor, and engineer, Archimedes understood **levers** and pulleys and why things float, and used this knowledge to build amazing war machines.

What he said

❝ Give me a place to stand and a lever long enough and I will move the Earth. ❞

How did he die?

Archimedes was killed by a soldier during the Roman invasion of Syracuse.

Find out more

This site tells the story of Archimedes' "Eureka!" moment: www.springboardmagazine.com/reading/eurekastory.htm

Eureka!

A legendary story tells how Archimedes realized why things float. King Heiron, the ruler of Syracuse, asked Archimedes to work out if his crown was made of pure gold. Later, in his bath, Archimedes realized he could measure the volume of the crown, and so its density, by putting it into a tub full of water and measuring how much water overflowed. It is said that he leapt from the bath, and ran down the street shouting "Eureka!" (which means "I have found it!"). This discovery led him to come up with what is now known as Archimedes' principle. The principle says that the upward push on an object in water is equal to the weight of the water that the object pushes aside.

Timeline

Born in Syracuse, Sicily

Killed in Syracuse

C. **287** BC

C. **213** BC

C. **212** BC

Helps to defend Syracuse against Roman attack

Archimedes studied levers and pulleys. He set up a system that allowed King Heiron to move a ship with his hands. He also built war machines to defend Syracuse from the Romans.

Archimedes' legacy

We use Archimedes' compound pulley to lift heavy objects and his Archimedean screw to raise water from one field to another. In maths, Archimedes worked out equations for the volume and surface areas of a sphere.

Robert Boyle

The Irish chemist and philosopher Robert Boyle was the first scientist to carry out logical and careful experiments to test his theories.

Boyle and Hooke

Boyle was born into a wealthy family at Lismore Castle, Ireland. He was educated at Eton College and in Geneva. In 1649, Boyle built a laboratory and began carrying out his science experiments. He wrote down the methods he used and the results he got, even if the experiment failed. In 1655, Boyle met Robert Hooke (⇨p13), who became his assistant. Together they designed an air pump that allowed Hooke to study vacuums. They showed that sound cannot travel in a vacuum and that air is needed for breathing and burning.

His most famous discovery, called Boyle's law, is an equation that relates the **pressure** and volume of a gas. In 1661, Boyle published *The Sceptical Chemist*. In his book, Boyle said that Aristotle's idea of the four elements (⇨p19) was wrong. Boyle suggested that everything consists of "primitive bodies" that combine to make different materials.

Did you know?

In 1667, Boyle invented the first anemometer — a device used to measure wind speed.

Find out more

Lots of fun facts at the Birkbeck College site dedicated to Boyle: www.bbk.ac.uk/boyle

More information about Boyle's extraordinary contribution to science can be found at: www.bbc.co.uk/history/historic_figures/boyle_robert.shtml

Timeline

Born in Ireland	Begins scientific experiments	Moves to London			
1627	**1638**	**1649**	**1661**	**1668**	**1691**
	Moves to Geneva to study		Publishes *The Sceptical Chemist*	Dies in London, aged 64	

The first chemist

Boyle was the first modern chemist. His idea of "primitive bodies" was the starting point for the modern theory of chemical elements. Boyle also established the idea that science could only be described by experiments. He did not believe anything unless he could do experiments to prove it.

How did he die?

Boyle died in London after two years of ill health a week after his sister's death.

Isaac Newton

English scientist Isaac Newton has become one of the most famous scientists of all time thanks to his discoveries and theories about gravity, moving objects, light, and mathematics.

What he said

66 No great discovery was ever made without a bold guess. 99

How did he die?

Newton died naturally, but his body contained a lot of mercury, probably from his experiments.

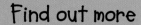

Find out more

This site has some simple explanations of Newton's laws: www.allworldknowledge.com/newton

Discover more about Newton's life and laws at: http://galileoandeinstein.physics.virginia.edu/lectures/newton.html

Motion and gravity

In 1661, Newton went to Cambridge University. He was forced to return home in 1665 when the university closed. Even then he spent his time thinking about maths and laws of nature. Newton worked out three laws to describe how objects move. These rules are now known as Newton's laws of motion. Famously, Newton began to think about gravity after he saw an apple fall from a tree. He realized that the apple was attracted to the ground by a force, and that it was the same force that held the planets in orbit around the Sun. He then worked out the law of gravitation. The laws of motion and the law of gravitation were published in 1687. In his studies of light, Newton discovered that white light consists of many colours, and he imagined that light is made up of particles.

Timeline

Born in Woolsthorpe, England

Becomes professor of maths at Cambridge

Publishes a book about light

| 1642 | 1661 | 1669 | 1687 | 1704 | 1727 |

Studies at Cambridge University

Publishes *Principia*

Dies in London, aged 84

Place in science

Newton's laws of gravitation and motion were important developments as they could be applied to objects in space as well as objects on Earth. Some experts think that *Principia* is the greatest scientific work ever written. Newton also invented the reflecting telescope and made important advances in mathematics.

Antoine Lavoisier

The French chemist Antoine Lavoisier made major discoveries in science and became known as the founder of modern chemistry.

Conserving matter

Lavoisier is best known for the law of conservation of matter. He showed that matter is not lost or gained when something burns. He also showed that solids get heavier when they burn because they react with oxygen in the air.

Timeline

Born in Paris

1743

1788

Names oxygen

Dies by execution in Paris, aged 50

1794

John Dalton

An English scientist who became a school teacher when he was just 12 years old, John Dalton is famous for his atomic theory.

The atom

The results of Dalton's experiments led him to believe that different gases were made of different sorts of particles, which he called atoms. Dalton announced his theory in 1803.

Find out more

Find out more about Dalton and atomic theory at:
http://atomictimeline.net

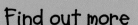

Timeline

Born in Eaglesfield, England

1766

1803

Gives a lecture on his atomic theory

Dies in Manchester, England, aged 77

1844

Michael Faraday

English physicist and chemist Michael Faraday made important discoveries about magnetism and electricity. He invented the electric motor and electric **generator**.

Ahead of his time

In 1821, Faraday found that a wire carrying electric current would move around a magnet. He soon built the first electric motor. In 1831, Faraday made use of **electromagnetic induction** to build a generator and **transformer**.

Find out more

Read about the life of this great physicist at:
www.bbc.co.uk/
history/historic_figures/
faraday_michael.shtml

Timeline

1791	1821	1831	1833	1867
Born in London	Invents the electric motor	Discovers electromagnetic induction	Writes the laws of electrolysis	Dies in London, aged 75

Max Planck

German theoretical physicist Max Planck began a whole new era of physics with his quantum theory.

Energy in chunks

Planck was trying to work out a formula for how much energy is given off by hot objects. He showed that hot objects release energy in tiny chunks. Planck called these tiny chunks of energy "quanta." He was awarded the Nobel Prize for Physics for his work in 1918.

Find out more

The official Nobel Prize website includes a short biography of Planck:
http://nobelprize.org

Timeline

1858	1892	1900	1918	1947
Born in Kiel in Germany	Becomes Professor of Theoretical Physics in Berlin	Reveals the quantum theory to the world	Awarded the Nobel Prize for Physics	Dies in Germany, aged 89

Marie Curie

Marie Curie was the first famous woman scientist. She discovered two important new elements and won prizes for her work on **radioactivity**.

New discoveries

Curie grew up in Poland but moved to France to go to university. At the time, women were not allowed to study at Polish universities. She studied for two degrees, in physics and mathematics, at the Sorbonne University in Paris. While she was a student she met and married Pierre Curie (1859–1906), a French scientist.

What she said

66 One never notices what has been done; one can only see what remains to be done. 99

Timeline

Born in Warsaw, Poland

Discovers polonium and radium

Awarded Nobel Prize for Chemistry

1867   **1880**   **1889**   **1903**   **1911**   **1934**

Marries French scientist Pierre Curie

Awarded Nobel Prize for Physics

Dies in Paris, aged 66

How did she die?

Curie died of blood cancer, caused by the chemicals she used.

Curie was interested in radioactivity, which had just been discovered. She discovered two new radioactive elements, called polonium and radium, after detecting high levels of radiation from rock ores. She was awarded two Nobel Prizes for her discoveries. She went on to become Professor of Physics at the Sorbonne.

Curie worked with radium for many years and developed **leukaemia**. When she died, she was one of the most famous scientists in the world.

Uses of radioactivity

Curie's work made great advances, but she never completely worked out what radiation actually was. Today, we know radiation is dangerous, but we also use it in industrial processes and in medicine to treat cancer.

Find out more

A short summary of Curie's life can be found at www.crystalinks.com/curie.html

The American Institute of Physics has a page dedicated to Curie and the science of radioactivity. www.aip.org/history/curie

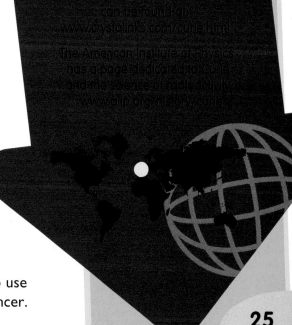

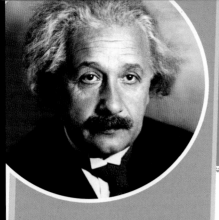

Albert Einstein

The physicist Albert Einstein revolutionized physics when he published his theories of relativity. His brilliant mind was far ahead of his time.

What he said

66 God does not play dice with the universe. 99

How did he die?

Einstein died from internal bleeding after a major **artery** burst.

Find out more

Simple information about Einstein's life: www.einstein-website.de

This is an archive of all the important documents produced by Einstein: www.alberteinstein.info

The American Institute of Physics has an Einstein page: www.aip.org/history/einstein

Relativity

Einstein studied in Switzerland for a degree in physics, before getting a job checking new inventions. In his spare time he studied the physics of light. In 1905, Einstein wrote a series of scientific papers. One paper was about the special theory of relativity. It stated that the speed of light cannot change, and that nothing can travel faster than light.

One of the papers contained the famous equation: $E = mc^2$. This equation showed that mass can be changed into energy. In 1916, Einstein published an advanced theory of relativity, called general relativity. His theories were proved correct in 1919, and Einstein became world famous. In 1933, Einstein left Germany because of the rise of the Nazis. He settled in the United States, where he worked at the Institute for Advanced Study at Princeton.

Timeline

1879	1902	1905	1916	1921	1940	1955
Born in Ulm, Germany		Publishes the theory of special relativity		Awarded the Nobel Prize for Physics		Dies in Princeton, USA, aged 76
	Starts work checking new inventions at the Swiss patent office		Publishes the general theory of relativity		Becomes an American citizen	

Place in science

By showing that mass can change into energy, Einstein began the development of the atomic bomb. In 1939, he encouraged the US government to build an atomic bomb, as he feared scientists in Nazi Germany would achieve the feat first. After World War II, Einstein decided that **nuclear weapons** should not be used.

Galen

A Greek who became physician to the Roman emperors, Galen was an expert on **anatomy**. His theories were followed by physicians for more than 1,000 years.

Life with gladiators

Galen studied many topics before taking up medicine. When his father died in 148, Galen went to Corinth, in modern-day Greece. He then travelled to Alexandria in Egypt to learn about medicine and philosophy. When he returned home in 157, Galen became surgeon to the gladiators in Pergamum, where he learned how to treat some of the horrendous injuries from fighting. In 162, Galen started work as a physician in Rome. He became well known and eventually worked as physician to the Roman emperors. He spent most of the rest of his life in the imperial court in Rome.

What he said

" Laziness breeds humors of the blood. "

Find out more

Discover more information about Galen at:
www.bbc.co.uk/history/historic_figures/galen.shtml

Another useful site:
www.zephyrus.co.uk/galen.html

Timeline

130	157	161	201
Born in Pergamum, in modern-day Turkey		Becomes physician to Roman emperors	
	Becomes surgeon to gladiators in Pergamum		Dies

Galen learned anatomy by carefully dissecting (cutting up) animals. He discovered **heart valves**, and that arteries carry blood. He treated many patients by letting out some of their blood. He knew how to take a person's pulse, and he performed delicate operations on the brain and eyes.

Galen's works

Galen wrote down everything he knew about the human body and medicine. In all, his work filled 129 volumes. Galen's incredible knowledge was used to teach medicine in Europe and the Arab world for 1,400 years.

Did you know?

Roman law prevented Galen from dissecting human bodies.

27

Andreas Vesalius

The Belgian physician Andreas Vesalius was the first person to make careful studies of the human body.

Challenging Galen

In 1537, Vesalius became a professor of anatomy. In the early 1540s, he studied the remains of dead people (that he got from executioners). His work led him to challenge the ideas of Galen (⇨p27). He published a book with accurate and detailed diagrams based on his studies of the human body.

Find out more

Discover more about Vesalius at:
www.bbc.co.uk/
history/historic_figures/
vesalius_andreas.shtml

Timeline

Made professor of anatomy and surgery

Dies on a pilgrimage to Jerusalem, aged 49

| 1514 | 1537 | 1543 | 1564 |

Born in Brussels, Belgium

Publishes *On the Structure of the Human Body*

William Harvey

Through careful experiments with animals, English physician William Harvey became the first person to show that the heart pumps blood around the body.

Discovery of circulation

Harvey experimented on animals to study the **circulation** of blood around their bodies. He criticized Galen's ideas (⇨p27) in a book published in 1628. At the time, other physicians still believed Galen, but Harvey's ideas were gradually accepted.

Timeline

Born in Folkestone, England

Publishes *On the Motion of the Heart and Blood in Animals*

| 1578 | 1609 | 1628 | 1657 |

Becomes physician at St. Bartholomew's Hospital in London

Dies, aged 79

Edward Jenner

English physician Edward Jenner discovered how to vaccinate patients against a viral infection called smallpox.

Cowpox and smallpox

Jenner began studying medicine at the age of 13 and trained to be a surgeon in London. At the time, smallpox was one of the biggest killers. Smallpox was related to cowpox, which was common in cattle. Milkmaids often caught cowpox from their cows, and Jenner noticed that milkmaids who had recovered from cowpox never got smallpox.

In 1796, Jenner took infected material from a milkmaid and infected a boy. The boy got cowpox, but soon recovered. Six weeks later Jenner tried to infect the same boy with smallpox, but the boy remained in good health. Jenner named his process vaccination after the Latin *vaccinia*, meaning "cowpox." Jenner was given money from the government to develop his **vaccine**. Vaccination may have been discovered years before Jenner, but he was the first person to make his findings public.

What he said

❝ ... the practice of producing cowpox in human beings will spread over the world. ❞

Did you know?

By 1980, there were no cases of smallpox anywhere in the world.

Timeline

Born in Berkeley, England

Returns home to work as a doctor

Dies in Berkeley, aged 73

1749　　**1770**　　**1773**　　**1796**　　**1823**

Goes to London to study surgery

Carries out the first vaccination

Find out more

The official site of the Jenner Museum in Berkeley, England
www.jennermuseum.com

More information about Jenner can be found at:
www.jenner.ac.uk/edwardjenner.html

Wiping out smallpox

In Jenner's time, there was no cure for smallpox. Some people tried to avoid catching it by deliberately infecting themselves with a mild form of the disease, but this was often fatal. Jenner's vaccination was much safer. In 1853, vaccination against smallpox was made compulsory in Britain, and cases of smallpox had dropped dramatically by 1900.

29

Louis Pasteur

French chemist Louis Pasteur made discoveries that helped to fight killer diseases. This included the process named after him – pasteurization.

A chance discovery

At the age of 26, Pasteur was already a professor. One of his interests was the fermentation process. He discovered that some micro-organisms make fermentation happen, and others stop it from happening. He also found that micro-organisms in the air make food stale. He predicted that micro-organisms cause diseases. He found that harmful micro-organisms in milk and wine could be killed by heating the milk or wine to 63°C for 30 minutes. This process is now called pasteurization.

What he said

" Fortune favors the prepared mind. "

How did he die?

Pasteur died after a series of strokes. He was buried in the Pasteur Institute in Paris.

Find out more

A short account of Pasteur's life can be read at: www.historylearningsite.co.uk/louis_pasteur.htm

Find information from the Pasteur Institute at: www.pasteur.fr/english/html

Timeline

Born in Dole, France		Founds the Pasteur Institute	
1822	**1862**	**1887**	**1895**
	Completes first test of pasteurization		Dies in France, aged 72

In 1880, Pasteur injected chickens with some old bacteria that caused a disease called cholera. The chickens only got a mild form of disease because the bacteria were old. When the chickens were given a dose of fresh bacteria, they survived. Pasteur had made a vaccine. He went on to develop vaccines to protect against other deadly diseases.

Place in science

Pasteur's germ theory and vaccines saved thousands of people from death. He founded the Pasteur Institute, a foundation for research into diseases and vaccinations, which is still making important breakthroughs today.

Joseph Lister

English surgeon Joseph Lister saved the lives of many people by developing antiseptics. These chemicals prevented infections during surgery.

Lister's life

Lister studied medicine at the University of London. In 1854, he moved to Edinburgh, Scotland, to gain experience under surgeon James Syme. Lister married Syme's daughter, Agnes, who became his lab assistant. Six years later he became professor of surgery at Glasgow University. Lister knew of the work of Louis Pasteur (⇨p30), who discovered that many diseases are caused by micro-organisms, and he tested Pasteur's findings himself.

Lister realized that infections after surgery were caused by micro-organisms getting into the body during surgery. He began using a substance called carbolic acid to fight infections. He put it on wound dressings, sprayed it into the air in the operating theatre, ordered fellow surgeons to wash their hands in it, and cleaned surgical instruments in it. Infections after surgery were dramatically reduced.

What was said

❝ I doubt whether the work of any other man achieved as much for the saving of life. ❞

(Sir Earnest Rutherford)

Find out more

Information about Lister can be found at:
www.historylearningsite.co.uk/joseph_lister.htm

Discover more about Lister at:
web.ukonline.co.uk/b.gardner/Lister.html

Timeline

1827	1856	1860	1860s	1895–1900	1912
Born in Upton, England		Becomes professor at Glasgow University		President of the Royal Society	
	Marries Agnes Syme		Develops antiseptics	Dies in Walmer, England, aged 84	

Modern antiseptics

In the early 19th century many patients died after surgery. Nobody knew exactly why, but they thought it was because "bad air" got into the wounds. In fact, standards of hygiene were poor because people did not know about germs. Lister's antiseptics helped improve cleanliness in hospitals.

Did you know?

Many modern antiseptics are based on the same substance Lister used – carbolic acid.

Sigmund Freud

Austrian psychiatrist Sigmund Freud developed new theories about the workings of the human mind and about human behaviour.

What he said

66 Time spent with cats is never wasted. 99

How did he die?

Freud was suffering from mouth cancer and asked his doctor to help him to die.

Hidden thoughts and dreams

Freud was an intelligent child, and shone at school. In 1873, he went to the University of Vienna to study medicine. He then started working in a hospital in Vienna, where he studied a disease called cerebral palsy. His ideas about mental diseases began to form while he worked in Paris with Jean-Martin Charcot (1825–93). Charcot studied patients with an illness called hysteria.

In 1886, Freud set up his own clinic in Vienna. He developed a new way of treating patients, called free association. In this method, Freud tried to get his patients to talk about unpleasant thoughts. These thoughts were buried in what Freud called the "unconscious mind". Freud thought that the contents of the unconscious mind came out in dreams. He came up with the word "psychoanalysis" for his method of working. In 1938, Freud left Vienna because of anti-Semitism (Freud was Jewish) to live in London.

Timeline

Born in Freiberg, in modern-day Czech Republic		Publishes *Studies in Hysteria*		Moves from Vienna to London	
1856	**1865**	**1895**	**1899**	**1938**	**1939**
	Family moves to Vienna		Publishes *Interpretation of Dreams*	Dies in London, aged 83	

Place in science

Freud was a controversial scientist. Some of his work was not very scientific. But psychoanalysis is still practised, and many of Freud's terms are part of our everyday language.

Sir Alexander Fleming

A fortunate accident led Scottish biologist Alexander Fleming to discover penicillin, the substance that changed his life and saved the lives of millions around the world.

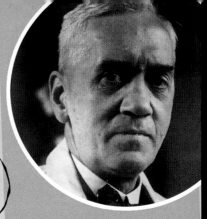

A chance discovery

From 1901, Fleming attended St. Mary's Hospital Medical School in London. When World War I started, Fleming became a captain in the Army Medical Corps. Millions of soldiers survived their injuries on the battlefield, only to be killed by infections by bacteria afterwards. After the war, Fleming tried to find a substance that would kill bacteria inside the body.

What he said

66 One sometimes finds what one is not looking for. 99

How did he die?

Fleming died from a heart attack.

Timeline

1881 Born in Lochfield, Scotland

1929 Publishes findings about penicillin

1944 Becomes Sir Alexander Fleming

1945 Awarded Nobel Prize for Medicine

1955 Dies in London, aged 73

In 1928, Fleming was growing bacteria in dishes. After returning from holiday, he discovered that he had accidentally left the lid off a dish. A type of fungi called *Penicillium notatum* had grown in the dish, and the bacteria around the fungi had died. He found that *Penicillium* killed other bacteria, too. Fleming named the bacteria killer penicillin, but he could not find a way to make it in large quantities.

Penicillin and prizes

In 1940, after the start of World War II, antibiotics were needed in large amounts. A team including Howard Walter Florey and Ernst Boris Chain found a way to manufacture penicillin. They shared the Nobel Prize for Medicine with Fleming in 1945.

Find out more

"Time" magazine's site includes of a summary of Fleming's life and work: www.time.com/time/time100/scientist/profile/fleming.html

Find out about Fleming and his discovery of penicillin: www.pbs.org/wgbh/aso/databank/entries/bmflem.html

33

Leonardo da Vinci

As well as being one of the greatest painters of all time, Leonardo da Vinci was a brilliant engineer and scientist who invented machines that were centuries ahead of their time.

What he said

66 The human foot is a masterpiece of engineering and a work of art. 99

How did he die?

Leonardo died in the arms of King Francis I of France.

Find out more

The Museum of Science site is full of interesting information: www.mos.org

Discover more about da Vinci at: www.bbc.co.uk/science/leonardo

Another great site: www.lairweb.org.nz/leonardo

Leonardo's life

Little is known about Leonardo's early life. He was educated in the workshop of Verrocchio, one of the great painters of the time. There he learned a wide range of skills, including drawing, painting, sculpting, and working with metals, wood, plaster, and leather. He left in 1472 and set up his own studio, where he probably worked until 1481. He then spent many years in Milan, Italy, but left for Venice after the French invaded the city during a war. In Venice he worked as a military engineer, designing ways to defend the city against possible attack. In 1516, he began working for King Francis I of France as a painter and an architect.

Timeline

Born in Vinci, in Italy

1452

Studies in workshop of Verrocchio

1466

Dies in Amboise in France, aged 67

1519

Leonardo's notebooks

Leonardo invented many things during his life. We know this from his notebooks, which contain sketches of many different machines. He designed city defences and war machines for attacking forts. He also invented weapons such as cannon, shells, and a tank. He drew a flying machine with flapping wings, a hang glider, a parachute, and a helicopter. He designed gears, pulleys, and hydraulic pumps. Leonardo also made important scientific advances in the study of light and the human body.

Thomas Newcomen

English engineer Thomas Newcomen invented the first steam engine, shown top right. It was the machine that powered the Industrial Revolution.

Life and works

Newcomen designed and built a steam-powered pump called a beam engine. Within a few years beam engines were pumping water from hundreds of mines in England.

Find out more

Find out more about Newcomen's invention at:
www.bbc.co.uk/
history/historic_figures/
newcomen_thomas.shtml

Timeline

Born in Dartmouth, England

Builds his first engine

1663 **1705** **1712** **1729**

Decides to build a
steam-powered pump

Dies, aged 65

John Harrison

British clockmaker John Harrison made precise navigation at sea possible with the invention of his marine chronometer, called H4.

Life and work

It took Harrison seven years to build his first chronometer, H1. He built three more versions until H4 was perfected in 1761. It was accurate to within a few seconds in a month.

Timeline

Born near
Wakefield, England

Completes H4

Dies, aged 83

1693 **1736** **1761** **1773** **1776**

Completes his H1
chronometer

Receives a government
prize for his work

George Stephenson

English mechanical engineer George Stephenson built the first passenger railway in Britain and developed steam locomotives to run on them with his son Robert (1803–1859).

What he said

66 The rage for railroads is so great that many will be laid in places where they will not pay. 99

How did he die?

Stephenson died of pleurisy, an infection of the chest.

New railways

From the age of 17, George Stephenson maintained and repaired steam engines at local mines, which allowed him to pay for his own education. Stephenson built his first steam locomotive in 1814. At the same time, he helped to develop iron rails that were strong enough to support heavy steam locomotives.

Timeline

1781	1803	1825	1829	1847	1848
Born in Wylam, England	Stockton and Darlington railway opens			Elected first president of the Institution of Mechanical Engineers	
	George's son, Robert Stephenson, born		Rocket wins the competition for Liverpool and Manchester Railway	Dies in Chesterfield, England, aged 67	

Find out more

Find out more about the life and work of Stephenson at:
www.cottontimes.co.uk/stephenson.html

More information can be found at this trainspotter's site:
www.trakkies.co.uk/railway-history/first-trains/george-stephenson

In 1821, Stephenson set up a company with his son Robert to build the locomotives for the new Stockton and Darlington Railway. The railway opened in 1825. Stephenson went on to build the railway between Manchester and Liverpool. The locomotive *Rocket* was built for this railway, which opened in 1830.

Stephenson's standard

George Stephenson was the engineer behind the rapid growth of the railways in Britain. He used the same distance of 1435 mm (4 ft 8½ inches) between the rails on all his railways. This is called the gauge, and it is the standard around the world. Modern trains run over bridges and through tunnels that Stephenson built.

Charles Babbage

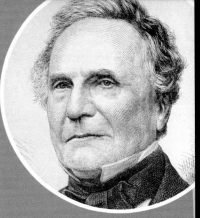

Nearly 200 years ago, English mathematician and engineer Charles Babbage designed mechanical calculating machines based on the same principles as modern-day computers.

Unfinished works

Babbage was frustrated by the errors he found in tables used for mathematical calculations. He decided to build a mechanical device that would calculate for him and print the tables. In 1822, he started to build his calculating machine, later called Difference Engine No.1. Work was held up in 1827 after Babbage's father, wife, and two sons died. One section of the Difference Engine was completed in 1832, but the machine was years from completion. It would have been incredibly complex, with 25,000 parts. Babbage was given government grants to help his work, but the funding was withdrawn in 1834.

What he said

❝ Errors using inadequate data are much less than those using no data at all. ❞

Find out more

Find out more information about Babbage's life at: www.bbc.co.uk/history/historic_figures/babbage_charles.shtml

A great site dedicated to Charles Babbage and his inventions: www.charlesbabbage.net

Timeline

Born in London, England	Professor of Mathematics at Cambridge University		Dies in London, aged 79		
1791	**1822**	**1828–1839**	**1834**	**1871**	
	Begins work on the Difference Engine		Begins to design the Analytical Engine		

Babbage then asked for more funds to build a new machine, called the Analytical Engine. He finished the design, but the funds never came so he did not build it.

Making the machine

Babbage's work was not recognized at the time, and he was criticized by his fellow scientists. In 1991, engineers at the Science Museum in London built a working version of the Difference Engine using Babbage's drawings.

How did he die?

Babbage died of kidney problems. His brain is on display at the Science Museum in London.

William Fox Talbot

British photographic pioneer William Fox Talbot developed a method of capturing images on paper, which became the basic method of photography throughout the 20th century.

Positives and negatives

Fox Talbot took his first photograph in 1835. By 1841, he had perfected his process. It used chemicals on paper that recorded "latent" (hidden) images. These images could not be seen until the paper was later developed.

Find out more

Find out more about Talbot at:
www.bbc.co.uk/history/historic_figures/talbot_william_henry_fox.shtml

Timeline

Publishes *The Pencil of Nature*, the first book illustrated with photographs

1800 — Born in Lacock, England

1846

1877 — Dies in Lacock, aged 77

Alfred Nobel

Swedish chemist, engineer, and inventor Alfred Nobel is the inventor of the explosive dynamite. He is also the man behind the Nobel Prize.

Invention of dynamite

In 1866, Nobel found that an explosive substance called nitroglycerine became stable when it was mixed with a substance called kieselguhr, which is like soft chalk. He called this new explosive dynamite. It was a huge success and made him a fortune.

Timeline

Born in Stockholm, Sweden

Dies in Italy, aged 63

1833

1864 — Nobel's factory explodes

1896

1901 — The first Nobel Prizes are awarded

Thomas Alva Edison

Possibly the greatest inventor of all time, the American Thomas Alva Edison developed many technologies that changed the world, including his famous electric light bulb.

A stream of inventions

Edison began working on the railways aged 12, selling sweets and newspapers on trains. At 14 he began to lose his hearing and was completely deaf in later life. From 1863, Edison trained and worked as a **telegraph** operator. The telegraph was used to send messages over a wire. He gave up work in 1869 to become a full-time inventor.

In 1876, Edison set up a laboratory at Menlo Park, New Jersey, USA, where engineers built and tested his inventions. Edison's inventions include the phonograph (a sound-recording machine) and the kinetograph and kinetoscope (which recorded and played moving pictures). In 1879, Edison invented the light bulb. In 1882, he set up the first electricity generating station in New York.

What he said

66 Genius is one percent inspiration and ninety-nine percent perspiration. 99

Did you know?

Americans switched off their lights for one minute on the day of Edison's funeral.

Timeline

1847	1863	1869	1877	1879	1931
Born in Milan, USA	Trains as a telegraph operator	Develops the stock ticker	Invents the phonograph	Makes the first successful electric light bulb	Dies in West Orange, USA, aged 84

Find out more

Find out more about Edison's life at: www.kidcyber.com.au/topics/edison.htm

Read an account of Edison's life and work at: http://memory.loc.gov/ammem/edhtml/edbio.html

New industries

Edison was a brilliant research scientist and businessman. He has a total of 1,093 patents (legal protection) for inventions in his name (or jointly) in the United States alone, and there were many more patents in Europe. In 1892, Edison founded the General Electric company, which is still a successful business today.

Alexander Graham Bell

Scientist and inventor Alexander Graham Bell is remembered as the man who changed the world by inventing the telephone.

What he said

66 Before anything else, preparation is the key to success. **99**

Did you know?

Bell refused to have a telephone himself because he found the ring too annoying.

Find out more

You can find out more about Bell and his telephone at: www.alexandergrahambell.org

Discover even more at: http://inventors.about.com/library/inventors/bltelephone2.htm

Work with the deaf

Bell was educated by his father and grandfather, and later studied at universities in Edinburgh and London. He learned speech therapy from his father, a trained speech therapist, and this fostered his interest in the science of sound.

In 1870, the Bell family moved to Canada so their son could recover from **tuberculosis**. The disease had killed his two brothers. Bell opened a school for the deaf in Boston and, in 1873, he became a professor at Boston University. In his spare time he experimented with sound. One thing he wanted to do was transmit (send) sounds over long distances using electricity, and he gave up work to concentrate on it. With his assistant, Thomas Watson, he finally solved the problem. Bell demonstrated the telephone for the first time in 1876 and became famous overnight. He continued to invent things (from giant kites to the metal detector) and to work with the deaf.

Timeline

Born in Edinburgh, Scotland

1847

1870

Emigrates to Canada

Becomes a US citizen

1882

1922

Dies in Canada, aged 75

A vital step

Bell founded the Bell Telephone Company in 1877 and made a fortune. The company built the telephone network that is the basis of communication around the world today.

Wright Brothers

Wilbur Wright (shown left) and his younger brother Orville (shown right) became famous when they built the first engine-powered aeroplane.

Kites and gliders

The Wrights' interest in flight is said to have come from a toy helicopter they shared as children. In 1896, Wilbur read about the death of gliding pioneer Otto Lilienthal, which made the brothers think about building their own aircraft. They began by looking at how birds fly and then studying the work of previous aviators, including Lilienthal. Then they built and flew a whole series of kites, model gliders, and full-size gliders.

Eventually the brothers built a glider with a home-made engine and propellers. Finally, on 17 December 1903, their aeroplane, *Flyer*, took off. Their first historic flight was just 37 metres (120 feet) long. By 1905, they had a plane that could stay in the air for more than 30 minutes. In 1908, they demonstrated their aeroplane in the United States and France. In 1915, Orville sold their aeroplane business.

What they said

66 For some years I have been afflicted with the belief that flight is possible to man. 99

(Wilbur Wright)

Find out more

You'll find lots of interesting information and images at:
www.first-to-fly.com

Further information about the Wright brothers can be found at:
www.thehenryford.org/exhibits/wright/default.asp

Orville Wright's own account of the first flight can be found at:
www.aero-web.org/history/wright/first.htm

Timeline

Wilbur Wright born in Millville, USA	Orville makes the first successful flight		Orville Wright dies, aged 76	
1867	**1871**	**1903**	**1912**	**1948**
	Orville Wright born in Dayton, USA		Wilbur Wright dies, aged 45	

Place in aviation

Flyer is perhaps the most important aircraft in the history of flight. Many people had flown in balloons and gliders before but the Wright brothers were the first to build an aircraft that could be controlled in the air by the pilot.

How did they die?

Wilbur died of typhoid fever, and Orville died of a heart attack.

Guglielmo Marconi

The Italian inventor Guglielmo Marconi was a pioneer of radio communications. He is famous for sending radio signals across the Atlantic Ocean.

What he said

❝ This new form of communication could have some utility [use]. ❞

Did you know?

The *Titanic* was one of the first ships to send a distress call by radio.

Sending messages

Marconi was born into a rich Italian family, which allowed him to carry out his experiments without needing to work. He heard about the discovery of radio waves by Rudolph Hertz (1857–1894), and he began experimenting with radio waves himself. His plan was to design a system for sending telegraph signals without wires. He set up radio equipment in the grounds of his family estate, and by 1895 Marconi had managed to send and receive radio waves.

Marconi then moved to London, where he received support from the British Post Office. In the following years, he increased the range of his radio signals, sending telegraph signals first across the Bristol Channel and then the English Channel. In 1901, Marconi became the first person to send signals 3,500 kilometres (2,100 miles) across the Atlantic. Marconi shared the Nobel Prize for Physics in 1909.

Timeline

1874	1888	1899	1901	1909	1937
Born in Bologna, Italy	Hertz discovers radio waves	Sends radio signals across the English Channel	Sends signals across the Atlantic	Awarded Nobel Prize for Physics	Dies in Rome, aged 63

Telegraph messages

Marconi did not invent radio communications, but he was the first to show that they could be used for wireless communications. He set up the Marconi Wireless Company, which began telegraph services in the United States and Europe, across the Atlantic, and for shipping.

Robert Oppenheimer

Robert Oppenheimer was a theoretical physicist and leader of the Manhattan Project. This was set up in the United States during World War II to develop an atomic bomb.

The Manhattan Project

Oppenheimer studied chemistry at Harvard University and then studied in England and Germany, learning from the top theoretical physicists of the time. From 1929, he worked at the University of California, researching physics and lecturing to new students. He was very popular with his students, who called him "Oppie."

What he said

66 I am become death, the destroyer of worlds. 99

Timeline

Born in New York, USA

Heads the Manhattan Project

Investigated for communism

1904   **1929**   **1942**   **1945**   **1954**   **1967**

Becomes professor at the University of California

Witnesses the first atomic bomb test

Dies in Princeton, USA, aged 62

How did he die?

Oppenheimer died from the effects of throat cancer.

Oppenheimer became director of the Manhattan Project in 1942. He set up a laboratory at Los Alamos in New Mexico and gathered a team of top physicists around him. They tested the first atomic bomb in July 1945. The next month two bombs were dropped on the Japanese cities of Hiroshima and Nagasaki, ending World War II. Oppenheimer was horrified at what he saw. After the war he opposed the development of nuclear weapons.

Find out more

Read an account of Oppenheimer's life at:
www.atomicarchive.com/Bios/Oppenheimer.shtml

Discover more about Oppenheimer at:
www.nndb.com/people/808/000047667

At what cost?

The success of the Manhattan Project meant that Japan surrendered without the United States having to invade. However, the dropping of the bomb brought about terrible devastation and enormous loss of life.

William Shockley

American physicist and inventor William Shockley revolutionized the electronics industry with the development of the **transistor**.

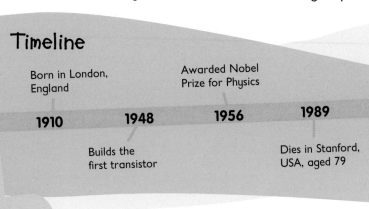

Early life

Shockley was born in England, but his parents were from the United States, and he spent his childhood in California. He studied at the California Institute of Technology and Massachusetts Institute of Technology. In 1936, he joined the Bell Telephone Laboratories. He studied crystals and electricity. During World War II, Shockley stopped his research on electricity. Instead he became research director of the US Navy's anti-submarine warfare group.

Did you know?
Shockley's transistor company was set up in an area of San Francisco now called Silicon Valley.

Find out more

Discover more information about Shockley at the Nobel Prize site: http://nobelprize.org/nobel_prizes/physics/laureates/1956/shockley-bio.html

Find out how transistors work at: http://inventors.about.com/library/weekly/aa061698.htm

Timeline

Born in London, England

Awarded Nobel Prize for Physics

1910   **1948**   **1956**   **1989**

Builds the first transistor

Dies in Stanford, USA, aged 79

Back at the Bell Telephone Laboratories, Shockley and fellow scientists John Bardeen and Walter Brattain made a transistor in 1948. Transistors control the flow of electricity in everything from radios to robots. Shockley soon developed a better transistor, called the junction transistor. Shockley, Bardeen, and Brattain shared the 1956 Nobel Prize for Physics for their work.

Shrinking electronics

Before the transistor, scientists used large devices called vacuum tubes to control the flow of electricity in circuits. The transistor was small, reliable, and cheap. It led to smaller electronic equipment.

How did he die?
Shockley died from prostate cancer.

Sir Tim Berners-Lee

English computer scientist Tim Berners-Lee transformed the world of information technology by inventing the World Wide Web.

Sharing information

Berners-Lee inherited his interest in mathematics and computer science from his parents. He studied physics at Oxford University, where he built his own computer. After working as a computer programmer, Berners-Lee moved to the European Organisation for Nuclear Research (CERN) in Geneva, Switzerland, where he worked as a software consultant. During the 1980s, Berners-Lee came up with the idea of linking documents on his computer to each other using highlighted words (now known as hyperlinks).

What he said

❝ Compared even to the development of the phone or TV, the Web developed very quickly. ❞

Find out more

Find out more information about Berners-Lee at:
www.w3/org/People/Berners-Lee

Another site about Berners-Lee and his work:
www.ibiblio.org/pioneers/lee.html

Find out how the World Wide Web works at:
www.explainthatstuff.com/howthewebworks.html

Timeline

Born in London, England

Begins working at CERN in Geneva

Awarded a knighthood

1955   **1976**   **1984**   **1989**   **2004**

Graduates from Oxford University

Invents the World Wide Web

The Web is born

In 1989, Berners-Lee realized that documents on computers all over the world could be linked together, forming a "web" of information. He chose the phrase World Wide Web (WWW) for his idea. The Web was launched onto the Internet in 1991.

Berners-Lee's idea was the starting point for the millions of websites on the Internet today. As the Internet has become available to people at home and work, the World Wide Web has grown into a gigantic resource of information. Sites are still based on Berners-Lee's software.

Did you know?

Berners-Lee built the first website, which was stored on a computer at CERN.

Glossary

anatomy Study of the structure and the parts of the human body.

artery Tube that carries blood from the heart to body parts.

bacteria Type of micro-organism. Many bacteria cause diseases.

black hole Region in space where gravity is so strong that not even light can escape from it.

circulation Movement of blood around the body, through the heart, blood vessels and organs.

diplomat Person who represents a government in a foreign country.

DNA Short for deoxyribonucleic acid, the chemical that stores genetic information.

elasticity Ability of a material to be squashed or stretched and then return to its original shape.

electromagnetic induction How movement and a magnetic field can produce electricity in a wire.

evolution How forms of life have developed on Earth over billions of years.

galaxy Collection of stars.

generator Device that produces electricity.

genetics Science of how characteristics (such as eye and hair colour) are passed from one generation to the next.

geology Study of the rocks that make up the Earth.

glacier Slow-moving river of ice that moves downhill from a mountain range.

heart valve Valve that stops blood flowing back into the heart after it has been pumped out.

leukaemia Cancer of the blood.

lever Simple machine used to move and lift things.

lightning conductor Metallic device that protects a building from lightning.

meteorologist Person who studies the atmosphere and the weather.

micro-organism Living thing too small to see with the naked eye.

nuclear weapon Device that produces vast amounts of heat by turning matter into energy.

pendulum String or rod, fixed at its top end and with a weight at its bottom end, which can swing from side to side.

plate tectonics Theory that the Earth's crust (thin outer layer) is cracked into large pieces (tectonic plates) that move slowly around.

pressure Push of a substance (normally air or water) on objects.

protozoa Single-cell life form.

quantum theory Theory that energy is emitted or absorbed in small chunks, rather than in a steady stream.

radioactivity Process of giving off radiation.

red blood cells Cells in blood that carry oxygen around the body.

seismograph Instrument that detects vibrations in the ground.

sunspot Cool, dark patch on the surface of the Sun.

telegraph Device used to send messages from one place to another using codes.

transformer Electrical device that changes the strength of an electric current using electromagnetic induction.

transistor Electronic device that can work as a switch or an amplifier (increase the strength of an electrical signal).

tuberculosis Disease of the lungs.

vaccine Substance that stops a person catching a disease.

vacuum Place where there is nothing, not even air.

X-ray Type of radiation used to photograph the inside of the body.

Index